D1626396

9112000414567

ALL ABOUT

Forces and Motion

LEON GRAY

raintree
a Capstone company — publishers for children

Raintree is an imprint of Capstone Global Library Limited, a company incorporated in England and Wales having its registered office at 264 Banbury Road, Oxford, OX2 7DY – Registered company number: 6695582

www.raintree.co.uk
myorders@raintree.co.uk

Text © Capstone Global Library Limited 2020
The moral rights of the proprietor have been asserted.

Original illustrations © Capstone Global Library Limited 2020
Originated by Capstone Global Library Ltd
Printed and bound in India

ISBN 978 1 4747 7720 9 (hardback)
ISBN 978 1 4747 7726 1 (paperback)

British Library Cataloguing in Publication Data
A full catalogue record for this book is available from the Britis

Acknowledgements
We would like to thank the following for permission to reproduce photographs:
Cover: Shutterstock: Nejron Photo. Inside: NASA: 36; NASA/CXC/MIT/C.Canizares, D.Evans et al), Optical (NASA/STScI), Radio (NSF/NRAO/VLA) 41; NASA/Sandra Joseph and Rafael Hernandez: 17; Shutterstock: AISPIX by Image Source 22, Yuri Arcurs 25r, Gregor Buir 19, Hung Chung Chih 44-45, Peder Digre 26, Max Earey 10-11, Iakov Filimonov 37, Lukiyanova Natalia Frenta 13, Germanskydiver 1, 34, 35, Iofoto 9, Ivanagott 15, Jabiru 4, Matthew Jacques 20, Tomas Jasinskis 28, Justasc 16, Dmitry Kalinovsky 31, Georgios Kollidas 40, Alexander Mazurkevich 18, MilanB 12, N Mrtgh 5, Mushakesa 43, Vitalii Nesterchuk 38, Nicku 14c, Nomad Soul 3, 29, Oliveromg 7, Alta Oosthuizen 21, Owl Mountain 23, Christopher Parypa 33, Pavel L Photo and Video 32, Pryzmat 24, 25l, Radu Razvan 6, Sippakorn 8, Sommthink 27, Vasilieva Tatiana 14b, Violetblue 39, Vladimir Wrangel 11b, Pan Xunbin 30; Wikimedia Commons: NASA 44, Lucas Taylor/CERN 42.

Contents

Feel the force

Forces make things happen. They push and pull on objects, speeding them up, slowing them down, and changing their direction. The forces that push and pull on objects on Earth are the same as those that keep the planets in orbit around the Sun.

Forces at work

If you have ever taken a ride on a roller coaster, you will know what it feels like to have forces pushing and pulling on your body. As you hurtle up and down, forces start to work. They make you feel heavier as you climb up the steep track, and lighter as you plunge down the other side. Forces push and pull on every object in the universe, from distant galaxies in outer space to the cells that make up the human body.

You can feel the effects of a force called gravity when you take a ride on a roller coaster.

Use the force

In ancient times, people used forces to build amazing structures such as the Egyptian pyramids and Stonehenge. They also invented simple machines, such as pulleys and wheels, to make work easier. At that time, however, no one really understood how forces worked.

Engineers in ancient Egypt used ramps, wheels and other simple machines to lift the heavy stone blocks used to build the pyramids.

SUPER SCIENCE FACT

Scientists measure forces in units called newtons, in honour of Sir Isaac Newton. One newton is the force that accelerates 1 kilogram (2.2 pounds) by 1 metre (3 feet) per second, each second.

Newton's Laws

In the late 1600s, English scientist Sir Isaac Newton came up with three laws to describe forces and motion. Newton's Laws of Motion paved the way for modern science.

Chapter One
Moving all the time

The world is constantly moving. Living things move around to find food. Machines, such as cars and planes, help people to travel more quickly than they can by foot. Our muscles provide the force to move our bodies around. Engines provide the force to move vehicles. Forces make things move.

Push and pull

Forces make objects move by pushing and pulling on them. Forces work all the time. Sometimes you do not even notice them. In fact, there are many forces acting on your body right now!

Gravity

A force called gravity is pulling you down towards the centre of Earth. You cannot feel it, but this invisible force is working all the time to keep your feet firmly on the ground. The ground pushes back with an equal and opposite force.

Cyclists must push harder on their pedals to cycle up a steep mountain because they are working against the force of gravity.

Out of balance

When forces balance, you cannot feel them. The two forces cancel each other out, so nothing happens. When forces do not balance, it makes objects move. Think about a tug-of-war, when two teams pull against each other on a rope. Each team tries to pull the other team forward by pulling harder on the rope. When the two pulling forces are the same, neither team moves. As one team tires, however, the two pulling forces are no longer balanced and the other team wins.

SUPER SCIENCE FACT

Engineers study the forces acting on structures such as bridges and buildings. It is important that the forces balance perfectly so the structures do not collapse.

A tug-of-war shows how pulling forces can make things move. One team must pull harder than the other team to win the contest.

Different forces

Different forces push and pull on objects to make them speed up or slow down. Some forces, such as friction and air resistance, are contact forces. Other forces act on objects without touching them. They include gravity and magnetism.

You can see the force of friction at work as a racing car skids along the track.

Friction

The force that acts on objects when they touch each other is friction. Every object, even something as smooth as a snooker ball, is covered with microscopic bumps and dents. When the ball rolls along the surface of the snooker table, the tiny bumps on the ball's surface rub against the bumps on the surface of the table. Eventually, the snooker ball will slow to a stop.

Air resistance

Another example of a contact force is air resistance. The air around you is not empty space; it is filled with molecules of gases such as oxygen and nitrogen. When you ride a bicycle, the molecules rub against your body and the bike. This rubbing force slows you down.

Forces at a distance

Some forces act on objects without touching them. They are called body, or non-contact, forces and include electricity, magnetism and gravity. These forces act on objects through invisible force fields that push and pull. An example is the magnetic field around a magnet.

The magnetic force of a horseshoe magnet acts at a distance to attract some iron screws.

Friction is often an unwelcome force because it slows down movement and wastes energy. But it is also very helpful. Without friction providing our feet with grip on the ground, we would not be able to stand up!

World in motion

As forces act on objects all the time, everything in the universe is always moving – the atoms and molecules that make up your body and even Earth itself, which constantly spins as it moves around the Sun.

Fast movers

Some things move very quickly. Earth moves around the Sun at more than 107,000 kilometres (67,000 miles) per hour. That is very quick, but light travels even faster than this. It moves at an incredible 300,000 kilometres (186,000 miles) per hour. Scientists think that light is the fastest thing in the universe.

The Bugatti Veyron may be the fastest car in the world – with a top speed of 407 kilometres (253 miles) per hour – but this is just a snail's pace compared to the incredibly fast speed of light!

Slow movers

Other things move much more slowly, so slowly that you do not notice them. A good example is Earth's continents. These giant landmasses are moving all the time, floating on a "sea" of molten rock beneath Earth's surface. But they are moving very slowly – on average, around 2.5 centimetres (1 inch) a year.

Muscle movement

Have you ever wondered how you move? Muscles provide the force to move our bodies. They pull on your bones to move your arms and legs so you can jump up in the air, move a chess piece and sprint along a running track. Large muscles have more pulling force than smaller muscles. This is why bodybuilders can lift much heavier objects than other people.

The strong, powerful muscles of an athlete provide the force to power him along the running track.

Understanding forces

The ancient Greeks were the first people to study forces. The Greek scientist Aristotle came up with the idea that forces push and pull on objects to make them move. It took another 1,600 years for scientists to take the next major step towards understanding forces.

When Galileo rolled a ball down a ramp, he found that gravity acted on the ball to speed up its movement.

Galileo's world

Italy's Galileo Galilei studied Aristotle's ideas and found that he had made some mistakes. Aristotle thought that forces always push and pull on things to make them move, but he was wrong. Galileo found that moving objects will move forever, but other forces speed them up or slow them down.

Constant motion

Galileo tested his idea by rolling a ball down a ramp. He found that it moved faster and faster because a force (gravity) made the ball speed up. When he rolled a ball along a flat surface, the ball rolled along at the same speed, but eventually stopped. Galileo realized that the ball stopped because a force (friction) slowed it down – otherwise it would keep moving forever.

Dropping cannonballs

Galileo did another experiment to test his ideas about forces and motion. He took cannonballs of different weights and dropped them from the Leaning Tower of Pisa. All the cannonballs hit the ground at the same time. Galileo proved that a force (gravity) pulls all objects down at the same rate no matter how heavy or light each object is.

SUPER SCIENCE FACT

In Galileo's time, religious people believed that God put Earth at the centre of the universe. Galileo used his knowledge of forces and motion to prove that the Earth moves around the Sun. When Galileo printed his ideas in a book, he was imprisoned for the rest of his life.

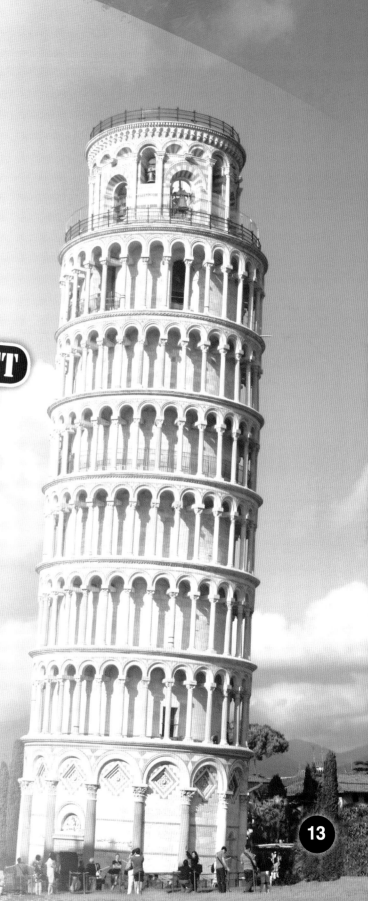

Galileo tested his ideas about the force of gravity by dropping cannonballs off the Leaning Tower of Pisa.

Newton's universe

Many people think that Isaac Newton is one of the greatest scientists who ever lived. His ideas changed the way people thought about the world around them.

As a boy, Newton did not take much interest in science. All this changed in 1661, when he went to study at Cambridge University.

Clockwork universe

Isaac Newton was born in England in 1642, in the same year that Galileo died. He studied the work of Galileo and other scientists and used mathematics to combine all their ideas into a few simple laws. Newton's Laws worked for every object in the universe, which he described as a giant "clockwork machine".

Newton used a prism to split white light into a spectrum of different colours.

Best-seller

Newton wrote his ideas down in a book, called *Principia*, which was published in 1687. In the first part of his book, Newton explained that three basic laws determine how objects move when forces act upon them (see pages 16–17). Newton then used these laws to prove that gravity also makes the planets move around the Sun (see pages 18–19).

Work on light

Newton also discovered that white light consisted of different colours. He suggested that light was made up of particles – an idea that Albert Einstein then proved some 200 years later.

SUPER SCIENCE FACT

Newton was a brilliant inventor as well as a scientist. In 1668, he used a mirror to build an extremely accurate telescope to study the universe. He even invented the cat flap so that his pet cat could get in and out of his front door without him having to open the door himself!

Laws of Motion

Newton's three Laws of Motion describe how things move. They are the same for all moving objects – from cars travelling along a motorway to the planets moving around the Sun.

First Law of Motion

The First Law of Motion says that an object will stay still or keep on moving at the same speed, unless a force acts on it. This law is about inertia. If you throw a baseball up in the air, it will fall back down. Forces act on the ball as soon as you throw it. Air resistance slows the ball down, and gravity pulls it back towards the ground.

When you throw a baseball, the muscles in your arm provide the force to accelerate it through the air.

Second Law of Motion

Newton's Second Law of Motion says that forces make objects accelerate. It can be written as:

Force (F) = mass (m) x acceleration (a)

Bigger forces make objects accelerate more quickly. The harder you throw a baseball, the further it will go. It also means more force is needed to make heavy objects accelerate. Try throwing a cannonball instead of a baseball!

Third Law of Motion

Newton's Third Law of Motion says that for every reaction there is an equal, but opposite, reaction. When you throw a baseball up into the air, the force from your hand pushes the ball upwards. The same force comes from the ball pushing on your hand – in the opposite direction.

You can see Newton's Third Law of Motion at work when a rocket launches into space.

SUPER SCIENCE FACT

In his Third Law of Motion, Newton explained how rockets work – hundreds of years before they were invented. The force of the rocket's burning gases are balanced with, or equal to, the force of the rocket moving upwards.

Newton and gravity

Before Newton, no one knew how or why the planets moved. Religious people believed it was the work of the gods, but Newton used his knowledge of maths to discover the truth.

Isaac Newton came up with his ideas about gravity when he saw an apple falling from a tree in his orchard.

Apple tree
One story suggests that Newton was sitting in his family's orchard and saw an apple fall from a tree. He wondered if the force that made the apple fall downwards might be the same force that made the planets move around the Sun.

Force of attraction

Newton proved that gravity pulled the planets towards the Sun in the same way that it pulled the apple to the ground. This force of attraction kept the planets in oval-shaped paths, called orbits, around the Sun. Newton then invented a new branch of mathematics, called calculus, to work out the shape and speed of these orbits.

Newton used maths to prove that gravity keeps the Moon in orbit around Earth.

Law of Gravitation

Newton found that the force of gravitational attraction between two objects depends on how heavy the objects are, and how far away they are from each other. Heavy objects have a much stronger gravitational force of attraction than light objects. But if the two objects are far apart, the force of gravity is much weaker.

SUPER SCIENCE FACT

Gravity causes the rise and fall of the tides. As the Moon moves around Earth, its gravity pulls at the water from the oceans directly below it on Earth. This creates a high tide. Another high tide occurs on the other side of Earth where there is less gravity, and so the water bulges outwards.

Chapter Three
Simple machines

Long before Galileo and Newton, people had been using simple machines such as ramps, wheels, levers, pulleys and gears to help overcome forces and make it easier for people to move objects.

Ramps and wedges

One of the first simple machines was the ramp (inclined plane). Ramps were used thousands of years ago to lift the huge stone blocks needed to build ancient monuments such as Stonehenge. Today ramps have many uses, ranging from screws to zips.

Prehistoric people used ramps and wedges to raise the stone blocks of Stonehenge into position.

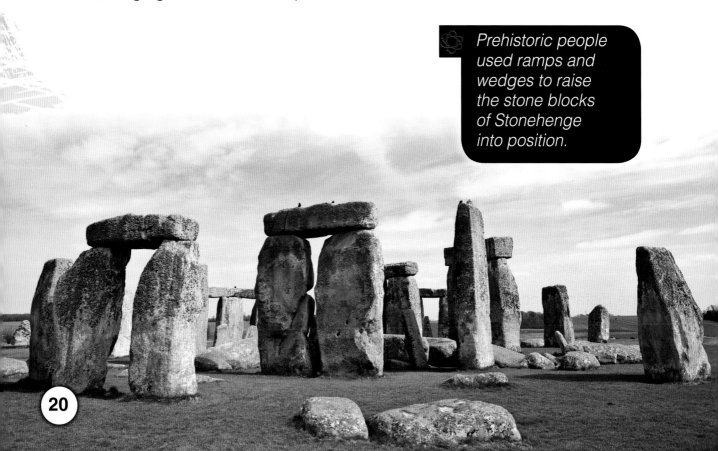

A mountain road is a perfect example of an inclined plane at work. The road winds up and down across the mountain, making it easier for people to drive up the steep slope.

A simple wood screw is a ramp wrapped around a central shaft.

Little effort, large effect

Like all machines, ramps increase the effect of forces so that a small effort produces a large effect. The force needed to drag a heavy stone block along a ramp is much less than the force needed to lift it straight up.

Mechanical advantage

The ramp gives a "mechanical advantage" because it increases the pulling force. However, you need to drag the block over a longer distance to lift the block the same height. Increasing the distance increases the mechanical advantage, but it takes longer to lift the load.

Ramps at work

Bolts and screws use "hidden" ramps in the form of the winding thread. Only a small force is needed to tighten the screw. The binding force of the screw and the wood is much stronger. Zips also use ramps to zip up rows of interlocking teeth. The ramp is in the zip slide, which forces the teeth to open and close with little force.

The wheel

Have you ever wondered why so many vehicles have wheels? Bicycles, cars, trains and aeroplanes all use their wheels to roll along the ground. Many machines also have wheels to make their jobs easier to do.

The first wheel

People who made pottery invented the first wheel in around 3500 BC. They used a turntable, called the potter's wheel, to shape clay into bowls and pots. Eventually, someone used wheels as rollers to make it easier to transport heavy loads.

Why wheels work

Sliding a heavy box over the floor creates a lot of friction, so it is hard to move. Rolling the box on wheels reduces friction, because only a tiny part of each wheel touches the ground at any one time. This makes the wheel an efficient way of moving something.

The wheels used to move vehicles, such as cars and bicycles, developed from the potter's wheel, which is used to shape clay into pots.

Wheels and axles

People first used wheels and axles on vehicles such as horse-drawn carts. An axle is a rod that connects two wheels. At first, the wheels rolled around a fixed axle, which was attached to the cart. But this created friction as the wheels rolled around the axle. People then invented the rolling axle, where the axle and wheels turned together to reduce friction.

The huge wheels of this truck have treads to roll over loose ground.

Levers

Every time you open a door, use a pair of tweezers or sit on a see-saw, you are using a lever. Levers work by magnifying and reducing forces to make tasks easier to do.

Different classes of lever

All levers consist of a solid part, such as a bar or handle, that turns around a fixed point called the fulcrum. Levers are grouped into three different classes.

Class 1 lever

A crowbar is a simple class 1 lever. In class 1 levers, the fulcrum is in the middle. The lifting force applied at one end of the lever is magnified at the other end.

A long crowbar produces a greater lifting force than a short one, but you have to move the long end much further than the load rises.

FORCE YOU APPLY

FORCE FROM THE LEVER

FULCRUM

Class 2 lever

A wheelbarrow is a simple class 2 lever. It magnifies the lifting force from your arms to pick up heavy loads. In this case, the fulcrum is at one end of the lever, and the lifting force is at the other end. This creates a magnified force to lift the load in the middle of the lever.

Class 3 lever

A pair of tweezers is a simple class 3 lever. The tweezers reduce the force from your fingers to pick up small, delicate objects. In this type of lever, you apply the force in the middle of the lever. The fulcrum is at one end of the lever and the load is at the other end.

FORCE YOU APPLY

FORCE FROM THE LEVER

FULCRUM

In class 2 levers such as this wheelbarrow, the fulcrum is at one end of the lever and the force you apply is at the other end. This creates a magnified force to lift the heavy load in the middle of the lever.

FORCE YOU APPLY

FULCRUM

In class 3 levers such as these tweezers, the fulcrum is the end of the tweezers and you apply the force from your fingers in the middle of the tweezers. This reduces the applied force to pick up delicate objects such as gemstones.

FORCE FROM THE LEVER

LIFE WITHOUT LEVERS

We use levers all the time, often without knowing it. The human body contains many levers – our arms, legs, hands and feet all help us to do jobs by magnifying and reducing forces.

Pulley power

All pulleys consist of a length of rope wrapped around one or more wheels. These simple machines are used to lift heavy loads.

Archimedes' pulley

A story tells of the ancient-Greek scientist Archimedes who used a pulley to lift a ship without any help. This story may be far-fetched, but it shows that pulleys can be used to lift heavy objects with little effort.

One wheel

A simple pulley has one wheel with a rope wrapped around it. Pulling on one end of the rope lifts the load on the other end of the rope. A simple pulley does not magnify the lifting force. To do this, you need a compound pulley.

Two wheels

Compound pulleys lift large loads because the lifting force moves further than the load. In a compound pulley with two wheels, it takes half as much effort to lift the load, and the lifting force moves twice as far.

A simple pulley is used to hoist a flag up a flagpole.

The problem with pulleys is that some of the lifting force is wasted because of friction between the rope and the pulley wheels. Another problem is the weight of the pulleys themselves, which reduces the lifting force.

Cranes lift heavy objects using a steel cable wrapped around a compound pulley. Each loop of the cable magnifies the lifting force of the crane.

Pulleys in action

Cranes lift and move heavy objects using a steel cable wrapped around a compound pulley. The pulley hangs off the main arm of the crane, called the jib. Each loop of the cable in the pulley magnifies the lifting force of the crane so it can lift heavy objects.

Gears

Gears are wheels with interlocking teeth that increase or decrease forces. Gears can also be used to change the speed and direction of motion. There are four main types of gear: bevel, rack-and-pinion, spur and worm.

How gears work

If the first gearwheel has more teeth than the second gearwheel, the second wheel turns faster but with less force. If the second wheel has more teeth, it turns slower than the first gearwheel but with more force.

Bevel gears

Bevel gears can be found in hand drills. These gears have two gearwheels that interlock at an angle to change the direction of movement.

Rack-and-pinion gears

Without rack-and-pinion gears, we would not be able to steer cars! Rack-and-pinion gears have a toothed wheel that runs along a sliding toothed rack. They change the rotation of the gear into movement along a straight line.

Power tools such as drills use gears to increase and decrease the turning force of an electric motor to drill through different materials.

Spur gears

Spur gears are two interlocking gearwheels. These gears are used to increase and decrease forces.

Worm gears

Worm gears have a toothed gearwheel that fits onto a cylindrical thread. They are used to tighten the strings on musical instruments.

Cycling made easy

You can see gears in action on bicycles. The large gearwheels near the pedals are called chain rings. A chain connects the chain rings to smaller gearwheels, called cogs, on the rear wheel. Choosing the right combination of gears makes cycling easier and faster.

A mechanical clock uses gears with interlocking teeth to keep the time.

LIFE WITHOUT GEARS

It is hard to imagine life without gears. Vehicles use gears to make travelling easier, faster and more efficient. Countless machines also need gears to work – everything from clocks and conveyor belts to washing machines and wristwatches.

Chapter Four

Forces and energy

Forces change the way objects move, but you need energy to make this happen. Energy exists in many different forms and can change from one form to another. Forces often occur when energy changes from one form to another.

> Houseflies use friction to climb up walls. Each fly foot is covered with tiny hairs, which increase the friction between the foot of the fly and the wall.

Friction force

Friction is the force that resists the movement of objects when they touch each other (see pages 8–9). There are two main forces at work when you try to move objects: static friction and sliding friction.

Static and sliding friction

Static friction is the stronger of the two forces. Static friction makes it hard to move a heavy object that is at rest (not moving), for example a heavy stone block on the ground. Sliding friction has an effect when an object starts moving. It is easier to push a heavy object when it is already moving, because sliding friction is weaker than static friction.

Wasting energy

Friction wastes energy. In a perfect system, all the effort you put into the system should be transferred into movement. Friction wastes some of this effort. You can feel this wasted effort when you rub your hands together very quickly. Your hands become hot if you rub them hard enough, because friction wastes some of the rubbing force and turns it into heat.

It is important to put oil into a car engine. Oil lubricates the moving parts and stops the engine from overheating.

G-force

Gravity is the force of attraction between every object in the universe. This invisible force is acting on your body all the time, pulling you down to Earth's surface and stopping you from flying off into space.

You can feel the effects of gravity on your body when you travel in a lift. When you start to move upwards, you feel heavier because the floor of the lift pushes against your feet. The reverse happens when you start to move downwards, and you feel lighter.

Measuring mass

Everything has a constant mass. Mass is a measure of the amount of material an object contains. Your body has a fairly constant mass, depending on how much you eat and how much you exercise.

How much do I weigh?

Weight is a measure of the force of gravity acting on your mass. On the Moon, your mass is the same as it is on Earth, but your weight is around one-sixth as much. Gravity on the Moon is less than it is on Earth, because the Moon has less mass.

Fighter pilots cope with huge G-forces as their planes twist and turn through the air.

Feel the force

The best way to feel the effects of gravity is to take a ride on a roller coaster. As you move up and down, the roller coaster speeds up and slows down. This affects the way gravity acts on your body, which changes your weight.

What is G-force?

G-force is the force you feel as a result of gravity pushing and pulling on your body. G-force pushes you into your seat as you travel up a hill on a roller coaster ride, making your body feel much heavier. G-force then pulls you off your seat as you hurtle down the other side of the hill, making your body feel lighter.

SUPER SCIENCE FACT

Fighter pilots feel huge G-forces as they shoot through the air at high speeds. As their planes twist and turn, pilots can feel up to nine times the force of gravity (9 g). This incredible force is enough to burst the blood vessels in their brains!

Freefall

Gravity acts on our bodies all the time. Usually we do not notice it because the ground under our feet balances the effects of gravity. You can feel the full force of gravity by jumping out of an aircraft.

Ready, jump!

As soon as you jump out of the plane, gravity accelerates your body towards Earth. In just a few seconds, your body accelerates to around 100 kilometres (60 miles) per hour. As you fall, your body rubs against the molecules that make up the air. This creates air resistance (drag), which acts against gravity.

Jumping out of an aeroplane is a good way to learn about the effects of gravity.

Terminal velocity

After around 10 seconds of freefall, the forces of gravity and drag balance. Your body stops accelerating and you plummet towards Earth at the same speed, called the terminal velocity. This is Newton's First Law of Motion in action – a moving object will continue moving at the same speed unless a force acts on it.

Speeding up

The terminal velocity of a falling object depends on its shape and weight. A typical adult skydiver falls at around 200 kilometres (120 miles) per hour. To create more drag, skydivers stretch out their arms and legs.

A skydiver reaches terminal velocity when the force of gravity balances the force of drag.

SUPER SCIENCE FACT

The world's highest skydive took place in October 2012, when Austria's Felix Baumgartner leaped from a balloon 40 kilometres (24 miles) above Earth's surface. Baumgartner reached a terminal velocity of 1,160 kilometres (725 miles) per hour as he plummeted through the thin air of Earth's upper atmosphere.

Moving in circles

If you have ever been on a loop-the-loop roller coaster, you will have felt a very strong force pushing you back into your seat as you loop-the-loop. This force, called centripetal force, stops you falling out of your seat, but only if the roller coaster is moving fast enough!

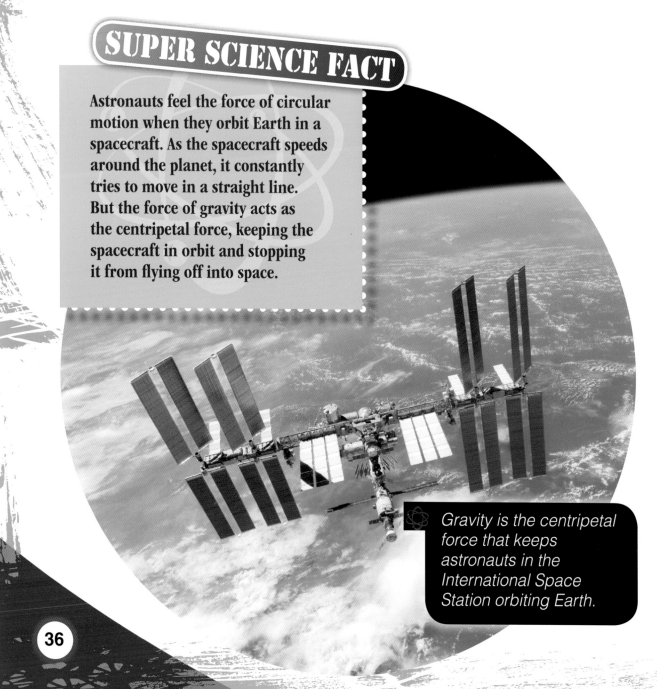

SUPER SCIENCE FACT

Astronauts feel the force of circular motion when they orbit Earth in a spacecraft. As the spacecraft speeds around the planet, it constantly tries to move in a straight line. But the force of gravity acts as the centripetal force, keeping the spacecraft in orbit and stopping it from flying off into space.

Gravity is the centripetal force that keeps astronauts in the International Space Station orbiting Earth.

Centripetal force

Centripetal force acts on any object that moves in circles. You can feel the effect of this force on a roundabout in a playground. As you spin around, your body keeps trying to move in a straight line. This is due to Newton's First Law of Motion (see pages 16–17). Your body appears to feel an outward force, called centrifugal force, which pushes you off the roundabout.

Deceptive forces

Centrifugal force does not really exist. The true force is centripetal force, which pulls you in towards the centre of the roundabout to keep you moving in a circle. This force acts through your body to keep you on the roundabout. Without it, you would fly off in a straight line.

Forces in action

Many different machines make use of centripetal force. For example, washing machines use centripetal force to separate the water from wet clothes.

Energy transfer

Energy is the ability to make things happen. Without it, there would be no forces to push and pull on objects to make them move.

Types of energy

Energy exists in many different forms. It can never be destroyed – it just changes from one form to another.

- Chemical energy is the energy trapped inside molecules such as oil and food.
- Electrical energy is the energy that comes from the movement of electrons through materials such as metals.
- Heat energy is the energy that comes from the tiny vibrations of atoms and molecules.
- Kinetic energy is the energy things have because they are moving. Objects have more kinetic energy when they move faster.
- Light energy is the energy from sunlight and man-made sources of light.
- Nuclear energy is the energy trapped inside atoms.
- Potential energy is the energy you gain when you climb a hill or stretch an elastic band.

Potential energy turns into kinetic energy when you bungee jump.

Your muscles turn the chemical energy locked away inside food into kinetic energy so you can move around.

Energy changes

The energy you use to swim or run around a football pitch is kinetic energy. Plants absorb the heat and light energy from the Sun to make food. In turn, this provides food for other animals, including people. When you eat plants and meat, your muscles convert the chemical energy in the food into kinetic (movement) energy.

SUPER SCIENCE FACT

Energy is measured in units called joules (J) in honour of the Scottish scientist James Joule, who established the link between different forms of energy.

Chapter Five
Fundamental forces

Newton's Laws of Motion work for most moving objects, but they do not work when objects start to move at speeds approaching the speed of light. Albert Einstein recognized this in his theories of relativity.

Albert Einstein developed a theory called relativity to describe objects moving at the speed of light.

Speed of light

Nothing can travel faster than the speed of light. Light travels through space at an incredible 299,792 kilometres (186,282 miles) per hour.

Strange light

Imagine you could travel 1.6 kilometres (1 mile) per hour slower than the speed of light. You might think you could catch the light. In fact, light still moves away from you at 299,792 kilometres (186,282 miles) per hour! If the speed of light never changes, Einstein worked out that something else must change to make up for it. He used complex maths to show that space shrinks and time slows down when objects travel close to the speed of light.

Einstein and gravity

Einstein expanded his ideas to explain how gravity affects space and time. He suggested that gravity is not really a force but a "warping" of space and time. Imagine space and time as a rubber sheet stretched out over a vast area. The mass of an object, such as a planet, bends the rubber sheet, so anything that moves near it will be attracted to it. This attraction is the "force" of gravity.

Light from stars in the Messier Galaxy takes 47 million years to reach the surface of Earth.

Invisible forces

Scientists use machines called particle accelerators to accelerate the tiny particles found inside atoms at near-light speeds. They hope these experiments will help them to understand the forces that hold the universe together.

This image shows the results of a particle collision inside the Large Hadron Collider near Geneva, Switzerland.

Particle accelerators

Einstein's theories of relativity show that nothing can travel faster than the speed of light. Using particle accelerators, scientists can accelerate particles up to 99 per cent of the speed of light and then smash them together. The force of these collisions creates a shower of new particles.

Predicting Einstein

The results of these particle collisions show that Einstein's theories of relativity are correct. Einstein used maths to show that mass can change into energy in his famous equation $E = mc^2$. When particles smash into each other, they change into new particles. This proves that mass and energy are two forms of the same thing. Einstein also showed that the mass of an object increases as it approaches the speed of light. Scientists have measured the mass of particles inside accelerators and found this to be true, too.

The strong and weak nuclear forces keep the protons inside the nucleus of an atom.

Fundamental forces

The experiments inside particle accelerators have shown that there are four fundamental forces: electromagnetism, gravity, the strong nuclear force and the weak nuclear force. All other forces come from these fundamental forces.

LIFE WITHOUT FUNDAMENTAL FORCES

The universe would collapse if fundamental forces did not exist. The strong and weak nuclear forces bind the nuclei of atoms together, while electromagnetism holds atoms together to form molecules. Gravity is the weakest fundamental force, but it works on a bigger scale, holding every object in the universe together.

Force for the future

In the last few hundred years, scientists have begun to understand how forces work. Science is moving forwards very quickly, so who knows what more we might discover about forces and motion in the future.

Forces in space

Another interesting area of research involves studying forces and motion in space. For example, scientists are studying the effects of zero gravity on the human body to see if people could eventually live in space.

Beating friction

Friction is the natural way to slow down something. As friction makes machines and vehicles waste energy, scientists and inventors are always looking for ways to beat it. For example, they have made trains that "float" on a magnetic field to reduce friction between the wheels and the track. These trains are called maglev trains, which is short for magnetic levitation.

Astronauts need to exercise in the weightlessness of space to stay fit and healthy.

Grand unified theory

Before he died, Einstein worked on a new theory to unite the fundamental forces. He called his idea the "Grand Unified Theory". Einstein did not succeed in his quest. Today, many scientists are still working to resolve Einstein's last great mathematical problem.

Maglev trains are very fast, speeding up to 580 kilometres (360 miles) per hour, but they are also very expensive to build. There are only two working maglev train lines in the world – one in Japan and the other in China.

Maglev trains beat the force of friction by "floating" on a magnetic track.

电力飞车

Glossary

acceleration how quickly an object speeds up or slows down

air resistance force that acts on things as they travel through the air. Air resistance is also called drag.

atoms tiny particles that make up everything in the universe

axle rod passing through the centre of a wheel or wheels

cells basic units of matter found in all living organisms

centrifuge machine that spins at high speed to separate mixtures

centripetal force force that keeps an object moving in a circle

electricity flow of electrons through an object

energy ability to do work

freefall falling through the air without a parachute or similar device so that the only force acting is gravity

friction force that opposes motion when one object moves over another object

fulcrum pivot point of a lever

G-force force equal to the force of gravity, for example 5 g is a force five times the force of gravity

gravity force of attraction between two or more objects

inertia tendency of an object to continue staying still or moving at the same speed

International Space Station artificial satellite that is used as an international research centre

lubricant substance, such as oil, used to reduce the effects of friction

magnetism property of some materials, such as iron and nickel, to push and pull on similar materials

mass amount of matter in an object

mechanical advantage measure of the force achieved by using a tool, mechanical device or machine system

microscopic something that is so small it cannot be seen by the human eye and must be looked at with a microscope

molecules combinations of two or more atoms

orbit curved path of one object, such as a planet, around another object, such as the Sun

particle accelerators machines used to accelerate tiny particles at speeds approaching the speed of light

plasma clear, liquid part of blood, made up mostly of water and proteins

relativity theories of Albert Einstein, which link the properties of space, time, gravity and the speed of light

speed how fast an object is moving

terminal velocity speed of an object in freefall when the force of gravity pushing down on the object equals the drag force pushing up

weight force of gravity pushing down on an object's mass

Find out more

Books

All About Physics (Big Questions), Richard Hammond
(DK Children, 2015)

DK Findout! Energy, Emily Dodd (DK Children, 2018)

Forces (Flowchart Science), Mary Colson (Raintree, 2018)

Forces and Motion (Essential Physical Science), Angela Royston
(Raintree, 2013)

Race that Bike!: Forces in Vehicles (Feel the Force),
Angela Royston (Raintree, 2015)

Websites

www.bbc.com/bitesize/articles/zqbm3k7
Learn more about gravity.

www.dkfindout.com/uk/science/forces-and-motion/laws-motion
Learn more about the Laws of Motion.